singing time!

grade 1

Step by step instructions for
ABRSM and other singing exams

David Turnbull

BOSWORTH 8-9 Frith Street, London, W1V 5TZ

Singing Time! Grade 1

To the Pupil

Almost everyone can sing. Singing brings pleasure to the singer – and often to the listener! It is perhaps the best way to learn about music. Your health will improve, too, because singing involves good breathing and muscle control. You don't have to buy a voice – you have one built in!

This book will help you to make the most of your natural singing gift. The songs in it provide you with a collection of music on which you can build.

Good singers don't just learn songs by ear. They must also learn how to sing at sight, so that they can learn new music quickly, and join singing groups. To do this, singers must understand the way music is written down. Knowing about rhythm, pitch, keys and intervals is just as important to singers as it is to instrumentalists.

You can learn a lot about singing from books like this, but you will learn much more if you also have a good teacher, and listen to experienced singers.

If you want to know more detail about music theory, you can use books in the *Theory Time!* series. References are given in the text. Practice for aural tests can be found in *Aural Time! Grade 1*. These books, by the same author, are all published by Bosworth.

To the Teacher

This book contains enough material for Grade 1 ABRSM Singing (1999–2000 syllabus).

Examination regulations provide that *any* printed edition of a song is acceptable, and that songs may be transposed to any key to suit the voice of the performer.

Grade examinations include singing at sight. Many beginners find this difficult, often because they don't understand the way music is notated. This book includes the necessary theoretical background. Songs are grouped by key, as without a knowledge of scales and keys no skill in sight singing can be achieved.

In Grades 1–5, **one** song must be chosen from **each** of the lists A, B and C. One traditional song must be offered, of the candidate's own choice. **All songs must be sung from memory.**

Songs included from List A are: *Home On The Range*, *Golden Slumbers* and *The Miller Of Dee*. From List B are *Noël Nouvelet*, *Quem Pastores* and *Die Nachtigall*. From List C are *The Cuckoo* and *The Crocodile*.

All other songs in Parts 2–5 are traditional songs, any one of which may be sung unaccompanied in the traditional song section of the examination — chord indications are included to help *in practice only*.

Further help with theory can be found in the author's books in the *Theory Time!* series, and with aural tests in the author's *Aural Time! Grade 1*. All these books are published by Bosworth.

David Turnbull

Music processing and text setting by Musonix Typesetting
Cover design by Miranda Harvey
Printed in the United Kingdom by Printwise Limited, Haverhill, Suffolk.

Basics

Benjamin Teall

Make sure you know everything in Part 1 before going on to Part 2.

Easysong part 1

Fairly slow

_f_ Here's the   start   of   a   use - ful   song.

Here is the music of the first part of a short song. It tells us about rhythm, speed (_tempo_), pitch, volume (_dynamics_), and the setting of words to notes.

Rhythm

1 Note values

(see Theory Time! 1 _pages 1–3)_

Notes in the music have oval **heads** – either black, or white. They have **stems**, going up or down. Two notes have **tails**. _The way notes are written tells us how long they are._

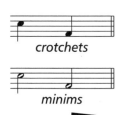

crotchets

minims

quavers

- **Crotchets** have black heads and stems without tails. _For now, one crotchet is worth one beat._
- **Minims** have white heads and stems without tails. A minim is twice as long as a crotchet, so it is worth _two_ beats.
- **Quavers** have black heads, stems, and single tails. A quaver is half as long as a crotchet, so one quaver is worth _half_ a beat. Sometimes, quavers are joined by their tails.

2 Bars and barlines

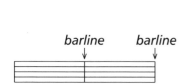

barline   barline

bar   bar

(see also Theory Time! 1 _page 6)_

Music is written in **bars**. A bar is the space between two barlines. Bars contain a set number of beats. Beats can be crotchets, or minims, or quavers.

3 Time signatures

Time signature

(see also Theory Time! 1 _pages 7–8)_

The **number** of beats in bars, and the **type** of note used, are shown by the **time signature**, written in the first bar.

Time signatures have two figures, one above the other. The **upper** figure tells us _how many_ beats there are in each bar. Here there are two beats in every bar.

The **lower** figure, 4, is a code, which tells us the sort of note used as the beat. 4 is the code for a **crotchet** beat. _Easysong_ has therefore two crotchet beats in each bar. A piece with a $\frac{3}{4}$ time signature has three crotchet beats to the bar, and so on.

Beats may be made up of shorter notes which together equal a crotchet. In Bar 1, both beats are crotchets. In Bar 2, the first note is a crotchet, which makes up the first beat. The second beat is made up of two quavers, worth a half-beat each. The last bar has a minim, worth two beats.

4 Tempo

The speed at which the beats follow each other is called the _tempo_ of the music. It is written at the start of the piece. The tempo marking for _Easysong_ is 'fairly slow'. Italian is often used instead of English. _See page 38 for terms and signs._

5 Counting beats and clapping rhythms
Clap the rhythm of ALL songs before singing, like this.

1. Count beats aloud to a steady pulse.
2. Say 'and' between each beat.
   The 'and' helps you clap quavers.
3. Clap the rhythm of the words.
4. Speak the words in rhythm.

Notice that the first beat of each bar has a natural accent: **one**–two–**one**–two.

Pitch
(see also Theory Time! 1 *pages 12–13)*

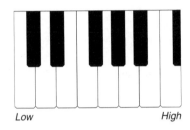

The *pitch* of a note is its lowness or highness. Use a keyboard to find out more about pitch.

Keyboards have white notes and black notes. Black notes are arranged in groups of twos and threes. The lowest note on a keyboard is the note on the left. The highest is the note on right.

1 Letter names of notes

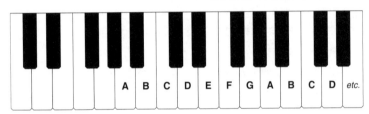

White notes are named alphabetically – A, B, C, D, E, F and G. Then the sequence is repeated.

Find the middle black note in a group of three. The white note to its right is A. The white note to the right of A is B. C, D, E, F and G follow, then the next set of A–G follows on.

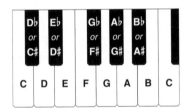

Black notes take their names from the white notes next to them. Each black note has a white note on both sides, so a black note has *two* possible names.

Look at the black note to the right of A. The black note to the *right* of a white note is called the white note's *sharp* (sign ♯). So the black note to the right of A is called A sharp. But this note is also the black note to the left of B. A black note to the *left* of a white note is called the white note's *flat* (♭), so the black note to the left of B can be called B flat, instead of A sharp.

Sharp and flat signs must be written exactly on the lines or in the spaces of their notes. They are written on the **left** of their notes.

2 Notation of pitch
Notes are written in musical notation on a five-line *staff* (or *stave*). Between the lines are spaces. Notes are written **on** lines or **in** spaces. Every staff starts with a **clef**.

Clefs
(see Theory Time! 1 *pages 13–15).*
There are several different clefs, but only one is used in this book in the singer's music. At the beginning of *Easysong* is a treble clef (𝄞). It is really an ornamental 'G'. It tells us that a note on the second line up of the staff is G. From it, we can work out the names of the other notes.

The last note on the music here is C, which lies below the five-line staff. It has a short line drawn specially for it, called a **ledger line** (or 'leger' line).

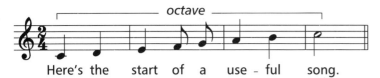

Here's the start of a use-ful song.

Easysong has two Cs in it, one at the beginning, and a higher one at the end. The C *below* the treble clef is called 'Middle C' because it is found in the middle of a piano keyboard.

The interval between the lower C and the higher C is called an **octave** – eight notes.

Notes on the Staff

In this diagram, you can see notes in the treble clef and also on the keyboard. You need to know these notes well.

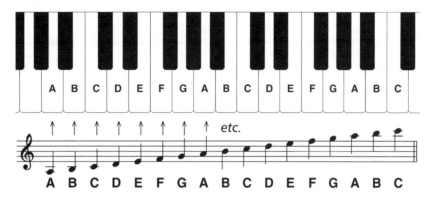

Most people start by learning first the notes E, G, B, D and F on the lines, and then the notes F, A, C and E in the spaces.

Dynamics

You need to know how loud or soft to sing. Dynamics are shown by letters and signs. For example, f means 'loud'. *(See page 38 for a list of terms and signs.)*

Intervals

Semitones and tones

(see also Theory Time! 1 *pages 18–19)*

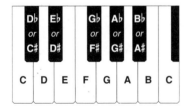

Notes next to each other on the keyboard are a *semitone* apart. The colour of the notes, white or black, makes no difference to this. Look at the keyboard again.

F is next to E, so between them is a semitone. D♯ (or E♭) is next to E, so the distance between them is a semitone. F♯ is next to F, so the distance between them is a semitone. (A semitone means a 'half-tone'. Two semitones make **one tone**.)

Scales and Keys

(see also Theory Time! 1 *pages 20–21)*

Scales are notes arranged in ascending or descending order. There are several types of scale. Major and minor scales are the most important.

The notes of *Easysong* are the white notes from Middle C to the C above. They are the notes of the **scale** of C major. Notes of the scale can be numbered as shown below.

Look at the scale of C major and the keyboard diagram on the next page.

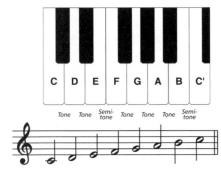

All major scales have this pattern of tones and semitones:

Tone – Tone – Semitone – Tone – Tone – Tone – Semitone (TTSTTTS for short).

C major is the only scale that can have this pattern without using black notes. Note 1 of a scale is called the **keynote**.

Music which uses notes from the scale of C major, written in any order, is said to be in the **key** of C major, so *Easysong* is in the key of C.

Before you sing the second part of *Easysong*, from bar 5, you need to know about notes followed by dots ('dotted' notes), tied notes and rests.

More about Rhythm

1 Dotted notes   (see also Theory Time! 1 page 5)
If a note is followed by a dot (as in bar 7 above), the length of the note is increased by half its original value. If a crotchet is worth one beat, the dot following it is worth half a beat. A dotted crotchet will therefore be worth one and a half beats.

2 Tied notes   (see also Theory Time! 1 page 6)

The length of time a note is sounded can be increased by tying a note to the note which follows it. The minim C shown here, worth two beats, is joined by a tie to a crotchet C. The tie mark means that the note must be sounded for *three* beats – two beats for the minim and one more for the crotchet tied to it. *Ties can only be used between two notes of the same pitch.*

3 Rests   (see also Theory Time! 1 pages 4–5)
Each type of note has an equivalent rest, which is the same length of silence as the note has sound. If a crotchet is worth 1 beat, a crotchet rest will also be worth 1 beat. A minim rest will therefore be worth 2 beats, and a quaver rest a half beat. Rests, like notes, may be dotted.

Some rests

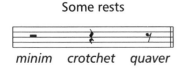

minim   crotchet   quaver

Words and Syllables
Words contain one or more units called syllables. The words of *Easysong* all have one syllable each except 'useful', which has the two syllables, 'use' and 'ful'. Each syllable *must* have at least one note, so 'useful' must have at least two notes. Syllables in a song have hyphens between them.

Words of songs have natural accents. Speak the words of *Easysong* and listen to the accents, which come naturally. Syllables can be marked with their natural accents by writing — over accented syllables, and V over syllables which aren't accented, like this:

—   V   —   V V — V   —

Here's the start of a use-ful song

Composers put accented syllables on accented beats – in two time, the first beat of each bar.

Part 2

Songs in C major

Breathing and Breath Control

Before you can sing *anything* with confidence, you must practise breathing and breath control. A good supply of air is like the fuel in a car's tank – without it, however good, the car cannot go.

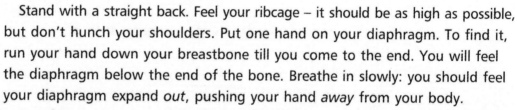

Stand with a straight back. Feel your ribcage – it should be as high as possible, but don't hunch your shoulders. Put one hand on your diaphragm. To find it, run your hand down your breastbone till you come to the end. You will feel the diaphragm below the end of the bone. Breathe in slowly: you should feel your diaphragm expand *out*, pushing your hand *away* from your body.

Breathing out is more difficult than breathing in. Control the escape of air so that you don't run out of breath before the end of the phrase. Here is an exercise to help. Breathe in for four slow beats. Then sing out for four beats. Do this several times. Then try counting to six. When this is safe, increase the number of sung beats to eight, then ten. If you get to the end of your breath too quickly, you are probably letting out too much air on one or more of the sung words. Sing to a feather or a candle flame and you will soon see where too much air is being used – the feather or flame bends.

When you need a new breath in a song, take it at a punctuation mark or in a rest.

Warming-up

Before singing any song, start work with warm-up exercises. Try these first.

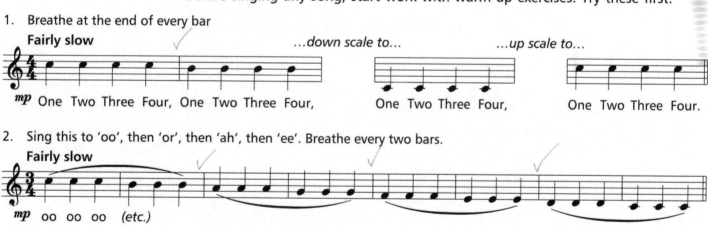

1. Breathe at the end of every bar
2. Sing this to 'oo', then 'or', then 'ah', then 'ee'. Breathe every two bars.

Melodic movement – steps and jumps

In *Easysong*, each note is next in the scale to the notes on either side of it. This type of movement is called **stepwise**. Most melodies, though, move by a mixture of steps and jumps.

Before singing a new song:
1   Clap the rhythm of the song, counting as you clap.
2   Look at any jumps, work out what they are, and practise them separately before starting.

fifth up

third down

Singing jumps

Jumps are measured by counting the number of notes from the first note of the jump to the last. The jumps in the carol below are a fifth, and several thirds.

The easiest way to sing a jump is to sing, quietly, all the notes of the scale from the first note of the jump to the last. Then sing only the first and last notes.

Now sing this traditional carol. Letters above notes are for the accompaniment only.

Unto Us Is Born A Son

Traditional Carol
Words by G. R. Woodward

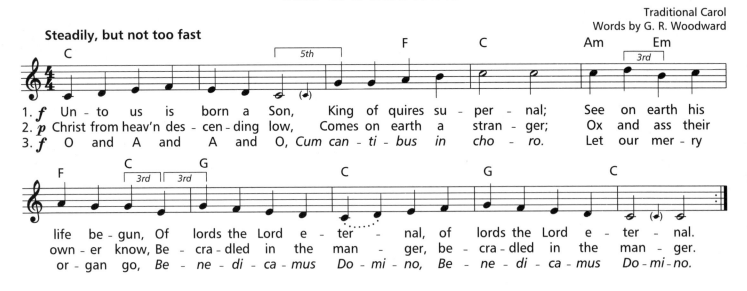

Semibreve

note   rest

The next song starts with an incomplete bar, so count 'One, Two' before starting. It contains semibreves. A **semibreve** is worth **four** crotchet beats.

Michael, Row The Boat Ashore

Traditional Spiritual

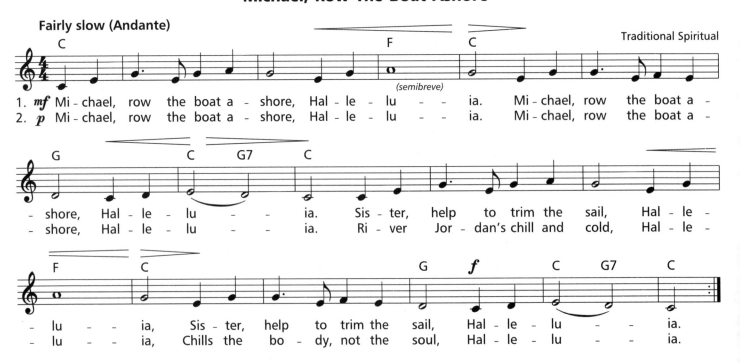

Semiquavers

The Happy Wanderer has some **semiquavers**, each worth **half** a quaver. The note and rest have *two* tails.

The Happy Wanderer

Traditional Austrian hiking song
Music by F. W. Moller, English words by Antonia Ridge

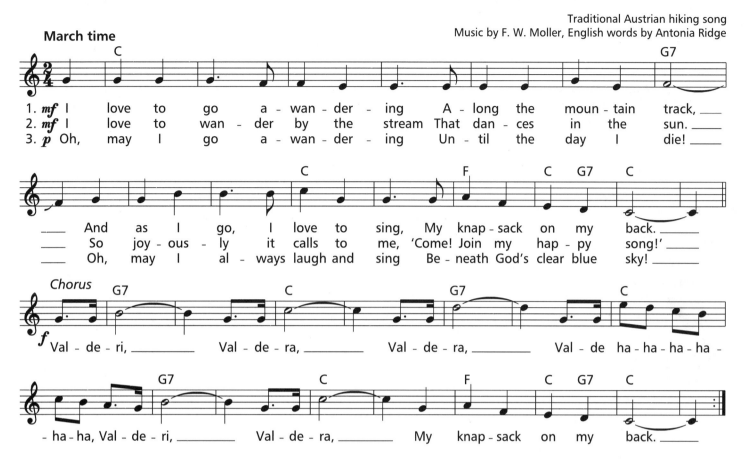

1. *mf* I love to go a-wan-der-ing A-long the moun-tain track, ___
2. *mf* I love to wan-der by the stream That dan-ces in the sun. ___
3. *p* Oh, may I go a-wan-der-ing Un-til the day I die! ___

___ And as I go, I love to sing, My knap-sack on my back. ___
___ So joy-ous-ly it calls to me, 'Come! Join my hap-py song!' ___
___ Oh, may I al-ways laugh and sing Be-neath God's clear blue sky! ___

Chorus

f Val-de-ri, ___ Val-de-ra, ___ Val-de-ra, ___ Val-de ha-ha-ha-ha-

-ha-ha, Val-de-ri, ___ Val-de-ra, ___ My knap-sack on my back. ___

Arpeggios

Notes 1, 3 and 5 of the scale, with the top keynote, form the **arpeggio** of the key. Arpeggios are useful for sight singing and as part of your warm-up exercises, so practise them in every key you meet. Here are words to sing with them (*signora* is pronounced 'see–nyaw–ra'):

Bel-la Si-gno-ra!

Where did you get that hat, where did you get that hat?

Memorising jumps

Start learning jumps 'by heart', by memorising ones you know. Many people do this by remembering starts of songs. Here are some suggestions, but make your own collection, and write them down on the music paper at the end of the book. Use jumps taken from songs you know really well.

3rd up — While shep-herds watch'd...

4th up — A-way in a ___ man-ger...

5th up — Baa, baa, black sheep...

6th up — My bon-nie lies o-ver...

Vowels and Consonants

Letters are either vowels or consonants. Vowels are **a**, **e**, **i**, **o** and **u** (these are discussed in Part 3). All other letters are consonants. Sing this exercise to help you pronounce consonants crisply – use your lips, teeth and tongue vigorously.

Pick two packs of pop – a – doms then crunch them with your cur – ry.   Pick two…
(continue up the scale)

Short'nin' Bread needs very crisp consonants.

Short'nin' Bread

Briskly (Allegro) ♩=120

Afro-American Traditional Song

1. *p* Three lit – tle child – ren, ly – in' in bed; Two were sick and the oth – er most dead!

Sent for the doc – tor; the doc – tor said: 'Feed those child – ren on short' – nin' bread.'

Mammy's lit – tle ba – by loves short' – nin', short'-nin', Mammy's lit – tle ba – by loves short' – nin' bread.

2. Put on the skil – let, put on the lid, Mammy's gonna make a lit – tle short' – nin' bread.

That ain't all she's gon – na do, Mammy's gonna make a lit – tle cof – fee too.

Mammy's lit – tle ba – by loves short' – nin', short'-nin', Mammy's lit – tle ba – by loves short' – nin' bread.

Part 3

Songs in F and G majors

C major is the only major scale that needs no black notes. All others need one or more. Songs can be written in any key. Singers need songs to be set in keys to suit the range of their voices. Many songs are most comfortable in the key of F major.

F major

The fourth note of F major is B flat.

Key signature

Scale of F major   Arpeggio of F major

Key Signatures

So that flat signs don't have to be written in front of every B, a **key signature** is written at the start of each staff. The flat sign applies to **all** the Bs on the staff.

Sing the scale of F major gently, *downwards* first then upwards. If the top notes are too high for you at present, just hum them. Then sing the arpeggio.

Extending your range

You can use arpeggios as a way of extending your range. Sing each of these twice.

Bel - la sig - no - ra   Bel - la sig - no - ra   Bel - la sig - no - ra   Bel - la sig - no - ra   Bel - la sig - no - ra

The next song needs to be sung smoothly. Try to sing bars 1–4 in one breath, as shown by the curved phrase mark above them. For other directions, see page 38.

Steal Away

In *Donkey Riding*, be careful to make the consonants crisp and clear.

Donkey Riding

(A 'donkey' is a small steam engine)

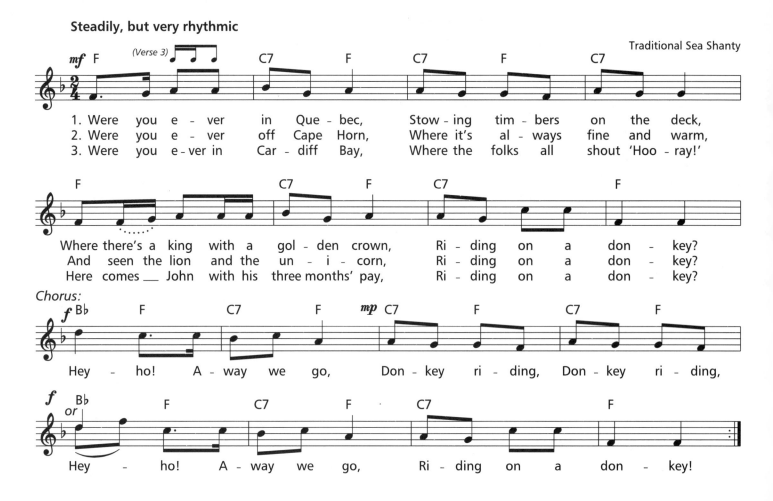

Steadily, but very rhythmic

Traditional Sea Shanty

1. Were you e - ver in Que - bec, Stow - ing tim - bers on the deck,
2. Were you e - ver off Cape Horn, Where it's al - ways fine and warm,
3. Were you e - ver in Car - diff Bay, Where the folks all shout 'Hoo - ray!'

Where there's a king with a gol - den crown, Ri - ding on a don - key?
And seen the lion and the un - i - corn, Ri - ding on a don - key?
Here comes ___ John with his three months' pay, Ri - ding on a don - key?

Chorus:

Hey - ho! A - way we go, Don - key ri - ding, Don - key ri - ding,

Hey - ho! A - way we go, Ri - ding on a don - key!

Accompaniments

Often, songs have piano accompaniments, like *Quem Pastores* on the facing page. The top line is for the singer, and the lower two for the piano. Count through any piano introductory bars, and find your starting note from them.

The next song is a Latin carol. Latin and Italian are good languages to sing, because of the purity of their vowel sounds. Pronounce:

- I like ee in *cheese*,
- E like the first e in *ever*,
- A like a in *father*,
- O as in *for*,
- U as oo as in *fool*.

Here are some other differences in pronunciation:

Quem	*kwem*		thus	*toos*
iam	*yam*		haec	*hake*
gloriae	*gloriay* (*-ay* as in 'play')		sincere	*sinchayray*
magi	*mahjee*		regi	*regee*
Aurum	*owroom*			

Remember to sing the melody over to 'lah' first, working out the jumps.
The 4 bar introduction ends with F, which is your starting note.

Quem Pastores

Traditional Latin Carol

The general meaning of the verses in English is:

1. The King of Glory is offered praise by shepherds, who had been told by angels not to be afraid.

2. Wise Men come, offering gifts of gold, frankincense and myrrh to the new-born king.

3. To Christ, God and King, given us through Mary, be praise, honour and glory.

Home On The Range needs rhythmic singing, to give the feeling of horse riding. It starts with an introduction for piano, and the top note of the right-hand chord is the C on which you start.

Home On The Range

American Cowboy Song

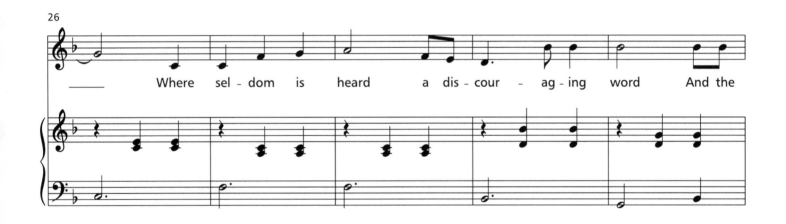

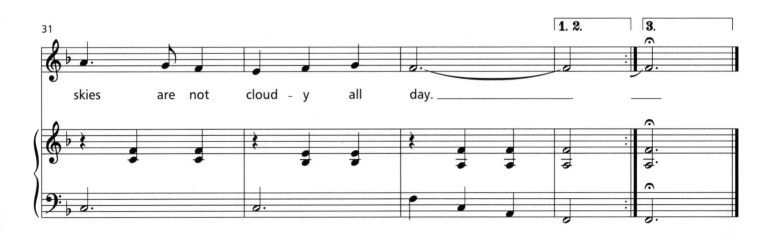

G major

(See also Theory Time 1 *pages 21–22)*

G major needs an F sharp instead of an F natural to keep the TTSTTTS pattern.

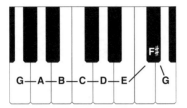

Scale of G major   Arpeggio of G major

Ar Hyd Y Nos

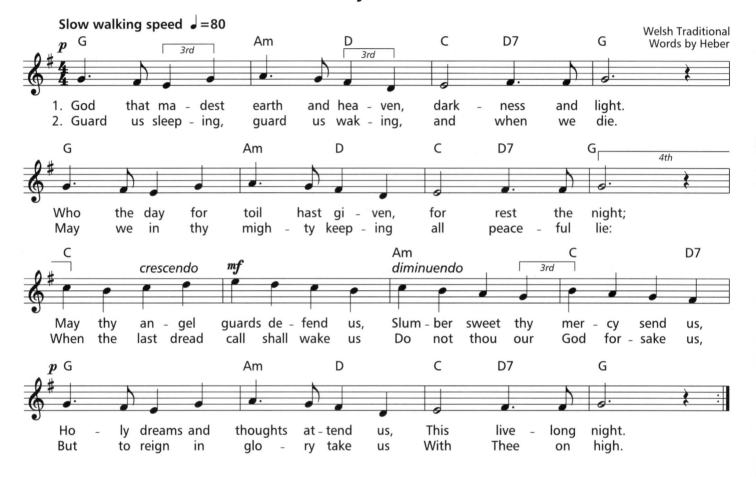

Welsh Traditional
Words by Heber

Slow walking speed ♩=80

1. God that ma - dest earth and hea - ven, dark - ness and light.
2. Guard us sleep - ing, guard us wak - ing, and when we die.

Who the day for toil hast gi - ven, for rest the night;
May we in thy migh - ty keep - ing all peace - ful lie:

crescendo   *mf*   *diminuendo*

May thy an - gel guards de - fend us, Slum - ber sweet thy mer - cy send us,
When the last dread call shall wake us Do not thou our God for - sake us,

Ho - ly dreams and thoughts at - tend us, This live - long night.
But to reign in glo - ry take us With Thee on high.

More about Time

1 Quavers as beats

So far, all the songs in this book have used *crotchets* as beats, so the lower figure of the time signatures has been 4.

Composers may choose to use *quavers* as beats. If so, the lower figure in the time signature is 8. Semiquavers become half beats, and crotchets are two beats. The song by Brahms on page 17 has three quaver beats to a bar.

2 'Simple' time

All the time signatures used so far are called 'simple' times, because the beat notes can be easily divided into two equal shorter notes. (For a song in $\frac{3}{8}$ time, see the next page.)

Die Nachtigall

(The Nightingale)

1. There sits a bird in a Christ-mas tree, call-ing and sing-ing out loud. What kind of bird __ can this one be? It is a nigh-tin-gale __ proud.

2. No, my friend, that is no nigh-tin-gale, No, my friend, take it from me, Nigh-tin-gales sing from a haz-el bush, Not from a Christ - mas __ tree!

3 'Compound' time

In some time signatures, the main beats cannot be easily divided into *two* equal shorter notes as in simple times. Instead the main beats can be divided into *three* equal shorter notes. These times are called 'compound' times. In Grade 1, you are only likely to meet ⁶⁄₈ time. In this, two *dotted* crotchet main beats are divided into three quavers.

Songs in compound time have a swinging feeling, as in *Looby Loo*, on the next page. This song has an unusual shape. It starts with a chorus, bars 1–8. All the verses are sung to the music of bars 9–16, and after each verse the chorus is sung again. The song ends after the chorus which follows verse 5. The instruction to end is the word *Fine*.

Looby Loo

3. Put your right foot in...   (Chorus)

4. Put your left foot in...   (Chorus)

5. Put your whole self in...   (Chorus)

Swing Low, Sweet Chariot

In *Bobby Shafto*, as well as all the changes in dynamics, you can make changes to the tempo. Slow down at the beginning of verse 3, and get slower still at *He's come back and married me.* Sing the last two bars faster and louder. Make sure all the consonants are really crisp by using the muscles of your lips as well as your teeth and tongue.

Bobby Shafto

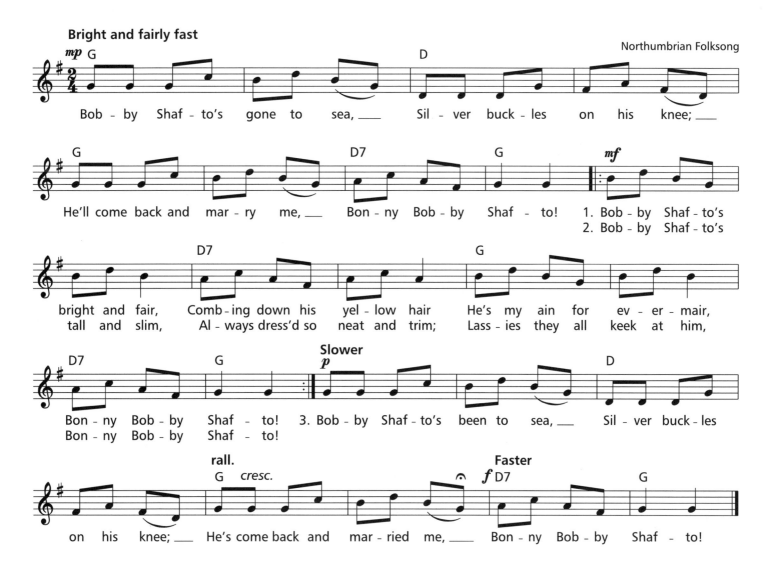

Stance and presentation

Stand as still as you can when performing songs. Keep your head up, and 'take in' the listeners in your look. Remember that in accompanied songs the piano part is important too, so stay still until the piano part ends. Look at the audience as much as you can.

Your shoulders should be high, but not hunched up.

If you need to use printed music when practising, hold it in both hands at a comfortable level – not too high.

Cuckoo

Music by Martin Shaw
Traditional words

Cuck - oo, _____ Cuck - oo, _____ Pray what do you do?

In A - pril I o - pen my bill, In May I sing night and day, In

June _____ I change my tune, In Ju - ly A - way I fly,

In Au - gust A - way _____ I must.

Cuck - oo, _____ Cuck - oo, _____ Pray where do you go?

Up high In - to the sky, Far a - way Ov - er the sea To Spain _____ I

fly a - gain; Day and night I take my flight.

Cuck - oo Good - bye _____ to you.

poco rit.

pp

21

Part 4

Songs in D and B flat majors

D major

D major uses two black notes, F♯ and C♯.

Scale of D major   Arpeggio of D major

Li'l Liza Jane

American Traditional

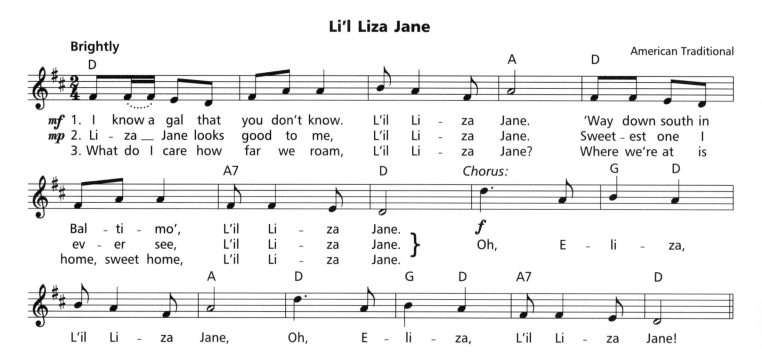

Barbara Allen is slow, gentle, and rather sad. Make the most of the expression marks and change the dynamics wherever indicated.

Barbara Allen

English Traditional

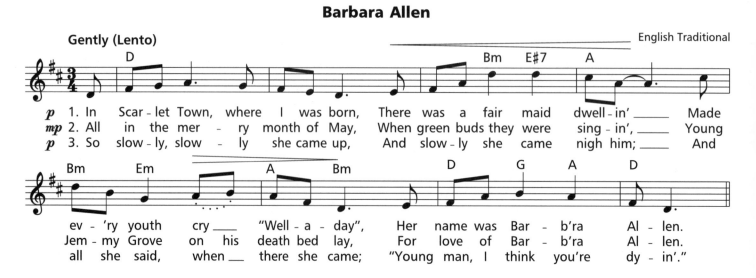

4. When he was dead and laid in grave,
   Her heart was struck with sorrow;
   "O mother, mother, make my bed,
   For I shall die tomorrow!"

5. "Farewell," she said, "ye maidens all,
   And shun the fault I fell in;
   Henceforth take warning by the fall
   Of cruel Barb'ra Allen."

B flat major

B flat major uses two black notes, B♭ and E♭.

Key signature

Scale of B♭ major   Arpeggio of B♭ major

Golden Slumbers needs to be sung gently, and with a lilt.

The piano introduction starts with an F, which is your starting note.

Golden Slumbers

English Traditional

1. Gol - den slum - bers kiss your eyes,
2. Care __ you know not, there - fore sleep,

Smiles __ a - wake you when you rise, Sleep pret - ty dar - ling
While __ I o'er you watch do keep; Sleep pret - ty dar - ling

do __ not cry, __ And I will sing a lul - la - by.
do __ not cry, __ And I will sing a lul - la - by.

Part 5

Going beyond major keys

So far, songs have been in major keys. However, you will often meet songs in minor keys, or which use other types of scale-like modes. You will learn more about these scales later in your musical studies, but here is a selection of songs to sing now.

I Will Give My Love An Apple

1. I will give my love an ap - ple with - out __ an - y core, I will give my love a
2. My head is the __ ap - ple with - out __ an - y core, My __ mind is the

house __ with - out an - y door. I will give my love a pa - lace where -
house __ with - out an - y door. My __ heart is the pa - lace where -

- in __ she may be, ____ And she may un - lock it with - out an - y key.
- in __ she may be, ____ And she may un - lock it with - out an - y key.

What Shall We Do With The Drunken Sailor?

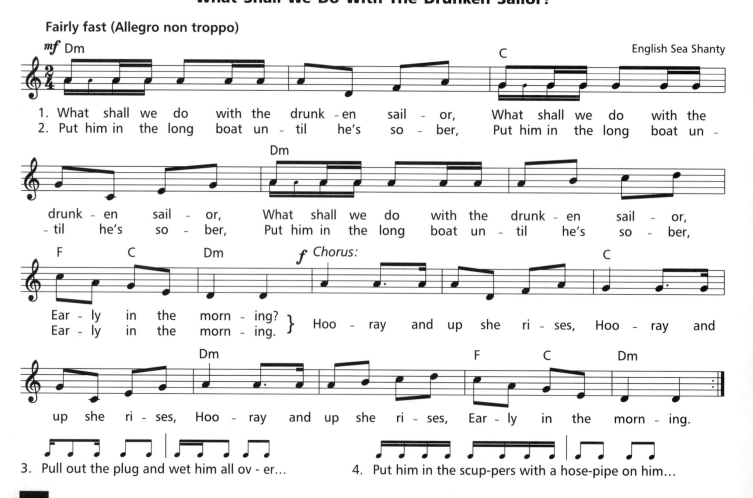

1. What shall we do with the drunk - en sail - or, What shall we do with the
2. Put him in the long boat un - til he's so - ber, Put him in the long boat un -

drunk - en sail - or, What shall we do with the drunk - en sail - or,
- til he's so - ber, Put him in the long boat un - til he's so - ber,

Ear - ly in the morn - ing? } Hoo - ray and up she ri - ses, Hoo - ray and
Ear - ly in the morn - ing.

up she ri - ses, Hoo - ray and up she ri - ses, Ear - ly in the morn - ing.

3. Pull out the plug and wet him all ov - er...   4. Put him in the scup-pers with a hose-pipe on him...

Noël Nouvelet

Traditional French Carol
English words by James Woodhouse

Steadily and rhythmically   *mf*

1. No - ël nou - ve - let, No - ël chan - tons i - ci;
1. No - el, sing No - el. Good peo - ple _ sing with glee;

Dé - vo - tes gens, cri - ons à _ Dieu mer - ci.   Chan - tons No - ël   pour
Thanks to God on high, who set - teth _ all men free.   No - el, No - el.   Let

le Roi nou - ve - let,   No - ël nou - ve - let, No - ël chan - tons i - ci.
all the na - tions sing.   No - el, sing No - el.   To greet the _ new-born King.

2. D'un oiselet après le chant ouis,
   Qui, aux pasteurs, disait: "Partez ici
   En Bethléhem trouverez l'agnelet."
   Noël nouvelet, Noël chantons ici.

2. Shepherds in the field, a small bird sang to them,
   "Where's your new-born lamb? Seek him in Bethlehem."
   Noel, Noel, to Bethlehem they run,
   Noel, sing Noel, to worship Mary's Son.

3. En Bethléhem Marie et Joseph vis,
   L'âne et le bœuf, L'Enfant couché parmi.
   La crèche était au lieu d'un bercelet,
   Noël nouvelet, Noël chantons ici.

3. In Bethlehem, Joseph and Mary see
   Donkey and ox, the Child lies inbetween.
   For Him no cradle, a hard crib lined with hay.
   Noel, sing Noel, sing, sing, Noel today.

English words reproduced by permission of the author.

G minor

G minor has the same key signature as B♭ major (B♭ and E♭) but, like all minor
scales, notes 6 and/or 7 may be raised by a semitone. In the case of G minor
this means that note 6 can be E♭ *or* E♮ and note 7 can be F♮ *or* F♯.

1   2   3   4   5   6   7   1'   7   6   5   4   3   2   1

25

The next song, *The Miller Of Dee*, is in G minor, but it is a jolly song. It needs to be sung lightly and crisply.

The Miller Of Dee

(In Grade 1 examinations candidates should sing only verses 1 and 2.)

The Crocodile

snap - ping and clapping of hor - ri - ble jaws, He search - es for food, and should he find your trail, He

wouldn't say no to a bo - dy like yours.

They say he can live for a great man - y years With his

croc - o - dile skin like an ar - mour'd car. Be - cause of his teeth there is no - thing he fears; When he's

seen in a zoo you are saf - er by far.

Slower *ad lib.*

And now that my stor-y is near-ly com-plete, Of the

colla voce

croc-o-dile's hab-its I'm sure you might dream; But re-mem-ber, the on - ly one you'll chance to meet   Is the

Tempo I

liz - ard who lives on the banks of a stream.

Part 6

Singing at sight

Singing at sight is difficult at first. Here is an example of the type of test you might have to sing at sight:

The key chord and key note of C major

In examinations, you will be played the key chord and key note, and then given half a minute to prepare the test. You will be played the key chord and key note again, just before you have to sing the piece. When practising, though, take as much time as is necessary to master the steps listed below – you will get faster with experience.

When you sing tests in exams, you may sing notes to the printed words, *or* to any vowel, *or* to sol-fa names. When practising, though, it is better to sing the words, as they help you understand the mood of the song.

- Work out the rhythmic pattern, including the introduction, by counting and clapping (see page 4). When practising you can, at first, write in the counting – it has been started for you in the example above. Clap the rhythm of the introduction then the words.

- Decide what key the piece is in, and on which note of the key it starts (it will not necessarily start on the key note). See if your starting note is played by the piano in the introduction.

- Most of the melodic movement will be stepwise, but there may be jumps. If you find a jump, work out its interval.

- Look at the dynamics and any expression marks, and be sure to include them.

- Sing the song slowly at first. When confident, sing it at its suggested tempo. In the exam, the accompaniment will be played by the examiner, who will therefore set the speed for you.

Using this approach, prepare and sing the song above, then continue with the other examples below.

Words: Anonymous

2. The winds were foul, the trip was long, Be‑fore we go _ we'll _ sing this song!

Words by Alexander Pope

3. To err is hu‑man, to for‑give di‑vine. __

Words by Lewis Carroll

4. Will ___ you, won't ___ you, Will _____ you, won't __ you, Will you join the dance? _____

Words: Thomas Hood

Steadily and not too fast

5.

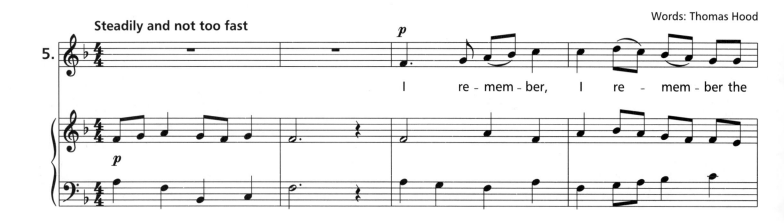

I re - mem - ber, I re - mem - ber the

house where I ___ was born.

Words by William Cowper

Lively

6.

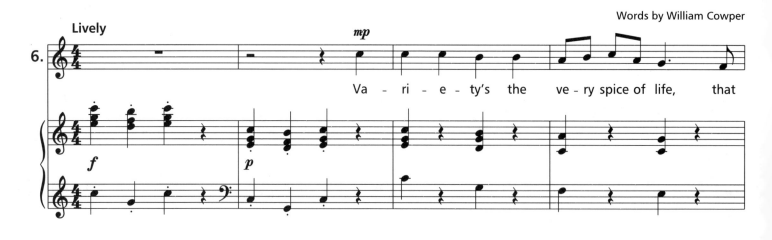

Va - ri - e - ty's the ve - ry spice of life, that

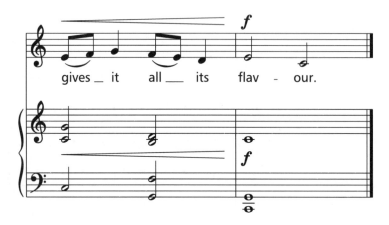

gives ___ it all ___ its flav - our.

Words by Lewis Carroll

7. Brightly

Twink - le, twink - kle, lit - tle bat! How ___ I won ___ der what ___ you're at.

Words: Anonymous

8. Briskly

What is this that roar - eth thus? Can it be ___ a mo - tor bus?

9. One _ crowd - ed hour ____ of glo - ri - ous life is worth ___ an age ____ with - out a name.

10. Old Joe Brown, he had a wife, She was all of eight feet tall, She slept with her head in the kit - chen And her feet stuck out in the hall!

11. Slowly and sadly

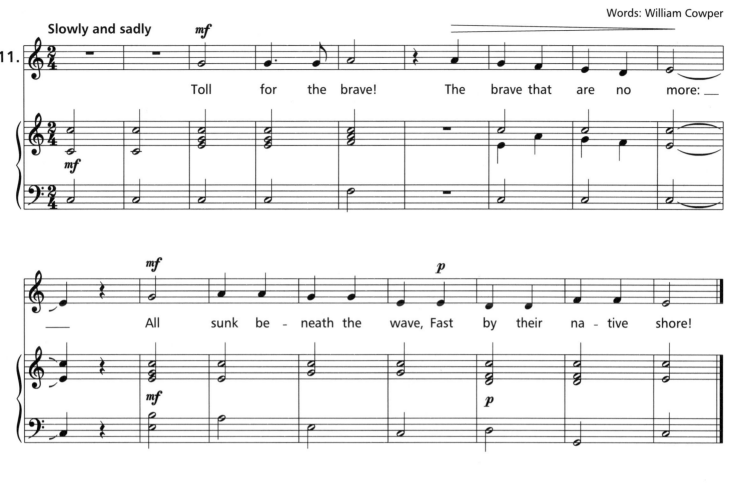

Toll for the brave! The brave that are no more: ___

___ All sunk be - neath the wave, Fast by their na - tive shore!

12. Slow

Wa - ter, wa - ter, ev - 'ry - where, Nor

(Stand quite still until the end)

a - ny, a - ny drop ___ to drink.

13.

"Will you walk a lit – tle fast – er?" said the

Whit – ing to the Snail, "There's a Por – poise just be – hind me and ___ he's

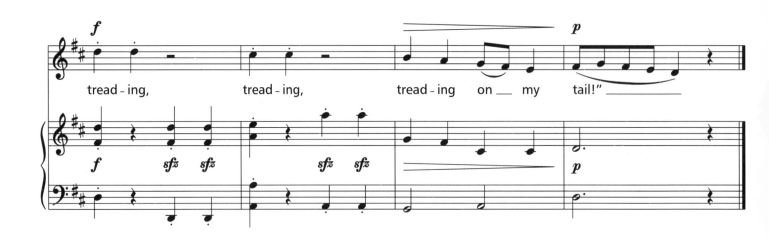

tread – ing, tread – ing, tread – ing on ___ my tail!" ___

Pronounce *Whiting* as *White-ing* and *Porpoise* as *Por-pas.*

Lastly, a longer example for you.

Note that a **semibreve** rest is always used to show a whole bar's rest, *whatever the time signature of the music.*

Musical terms and signs

Tempo

a tempo	in tempo
adagio	slow, leisurely
allegro	fairly fast
allegretto	fairly fast, but less than *allegro*
andante	moderate walking pace
lento	slow
moderato	at a moderate speed

Dynamics

forte	*f*	loud
fortissimo	*ff*	very loud
mezzoforte	*mf*	moderately loud
mezzopiano	*mp*	moderately quiet
piano	*p*	quiet
pianissimo	*pp*	very quiet

Changes to Tempo

accelerando	getting faster gradually
rallentando (rall.)	getting slower gradually
ritardando (rit.)	getting slower gradually
ritenuto (rit.)	holding back

Changes to Dynamics

crescendo (cresc.)	⊏	getting gradually louder
decrescendo (decresc.)		getting gradually quieter
diminuendo (dim.)	⊐	getting gradually quieter

Manner of Performance

legato	♩ ♩ ♩	smoothly
staccato	♩ ♩	sharp, detached
	♩ ♩	accented notes
	𝄐	pause

Performance Instructions

‖:	:‖	repeat the music between these bar lines
da capo	D.C.	repeat from the beginning
dal segno	D.S.	repeat from the 𝄋 sign
Fine		end
♩=60		A speed of 60 crotchets per minute.

The author wishes to record his thanks to

Paul Dean, for his assistance with the English paraphrase of *Quem Pastores*;
Lesley Rutherford of Bosworth/Music Sales for expert editing;
Paul Terry of Musonix, for advice and admirable typesetting;
Diana Turnbull, for many hours of help with text and proof-reading.

Name. Benjamin

Michaelmas Practice checklist

Week	1	2	3	4	5	6	7	8	9	10
Monday										
Tuesday										
Wednesday										
Thursday										
Friday										
Saturday										

Lent Practice checklist

Week	1	2	3	4	5	6	7	8	9	10
Monday										
Tuesday										
Wednesday										
Thursday										
Friday										
Saturday										

Summer Practice checklist

Week	1	2	3	4	5	6	7	8	9	10
Monday										
Tuesday										
Wednesday										
Thursday										
Friday										
Saturday										

Index of songs

Use the staves below to write down the openings of tunes you choose to help you remember intervals (see page 9).

Also in this series:

Aural Time!

Practice Tests for ABRSM and other exams

Like most musical skills, aural awareness needs regular training and practice. Aural work should be part of every lesson; teachers will find these books useful as supplementary material for practice in lessons, and ideal as preparation for all instrumental exams. The piano accompaniments to all tests have been kept simple.

Grade 1 BOE004796
Grade 2 BOE004797
Grade 3 BOE004798
Grade 4 BOE004799
Grade 5 BOE004800   Pupil's Book BOE004909 (Grades 4/5)
Grade 6 BOE004921   Pupil's Book BOE004924   CD of 99 examples BOE004921CD
Grade 7 BOE004922   Pupil's Book BOE004931   CD of 99 examples BOE004922CD
Grade 8 BOE004923   Pupil's Book BOE004929

Theory Time!

Step-by-step instruction for ABRSM and other exams

The principles of theory covered in the clearest possible way for people new to music. Ideal preparation for exams or as part of a general music education. Explains everything you need to know at each level, checking understanding with frequent tests. Answers are provided.

Grade 1 BOE004868
Grade 2 BOE004869
Grade 3 BOE004870
Grade 4 BOE004907
Grade 5 BOE004908

Scale Time!

A step-by-step approach to scales, arpeggios and broken chords

Scales are essential to the development of a fluent piano technique. The gradual approach in this book towards learning scales – with plenty of hints and tips – is ideal for exams as well as for general technique.

Grade 1 BOE004992
Grade 2 BOE004996
Grade 3 BOE004997
Grade 4 BOE004998
Grade 5 BOE005001
Grade 6 BOE005010

Bosworth
8-9 Frith Street, London W1V 5TZ
Exclusive distributors:
Music Sales Limited, Newmarket Road, Bury St Edmunds, Suffolk IP33 3YB